To our dear Rad... ...nda Happy
Birthday, Loads ...

Blessings on the flowers
Blessings on the fruit
Blessings on the leaf and stem
Blessings on the Root

First published in 1999
This revised paperback edition
© Wooden Books Ltd 2002 AD

Published by Wooden Books Ltd.
Walkmill, Cascob, Presteigne, Powys, Wales

British Library Cataloguing in Publication Data
Kindred, G.
A Hedgerow Cookbook

ISBN 1 904263 03 8

Printed and bound in Great Britain
by The Cromwell Press, Trowbridge

A HEDGEROW COOKBOOK

written & illustrated by

Glennie Kindred

*For my mum, Margaret Newman,
with appreciation of all the love and encouragement
she has always given me, and for my daughter, May.*

*This book is dedicated to Mother Earth in gratitude
for all her abundant gifts.*

*Remember!
It is your responsibility to use a good field guide.
Never ever eat a plant you are not entirely sure of!*

INTRODUCTION

Hedgerow cookery is an experience, an experiment, and a delight for all those interested in our native plants, country-lore, history, herbal medicines, and above all, food.

I use 'hedgerow' as a loose term, to include plants found in meadows and woodlands, and garden escapes which may be found wherever humans have inhabited in the past or present.

If you have a garden, let a bit of the wilderness in, and put aside areas where edible wild plants can grow. Many of these will thrive in shady places and in poor soils, along the hedgerows of your garden, and can be harvested as and when needed. No garden is without weeds, but if you eat them as well, then 'weeding' becomes 'harvesting'. Horticulture has encouraged us to undervalue our native wild flowers, but by introducing native edible plants into your garden, you can always find something to add to salads, soups and stir-fries. Importantly, those freshly picked leaves, shoots and flowers will be bursting with fresh vitamins and minerals, long gone from vegetables which have sat for days in shops. I have also included some garden plants which are worth growing for their food value.

Knowing which plants are edible, where to find them and when to find them, brings a deeper connection to our natural world, and brings you full circle to the knowledge of our ancestors.

Derbyshire 2002

HEDGEROW COOKERY
guidelines and foraging tips

Hedgerow cookery is not a survival test, it is about having the courage to experiment with the food you eat. Although your knowledge may prove useful to you one day, there is no need for the whole meal to come from the wild. Use it more as an exciting addition to your usual food. In the past 'pot herbs' were edible leaves added to soups and stews, collected from the wild or encouraged to grow in the kitchen garden.

I have included in this book *basic recipes* which leave the way open for your own interpretations and flair. Combining food from the wild with food you are more familiar with will help you integrate the new experimental tastes into your recipes. When walking, travelling and camping, your knowledge will bring invaluable additions to your food.

The book has four sections: Spring, Summer, Autumn and Winter, with plants and recipes for each season as well as basic recipes which can be used at any time of year. Remember to check ahead for seasonal overlaps. With so many plants to choose from, and the ever changing seasonal varieties, hedgerow cookery opens many doors for a varied and interesting source of free tasty food.

When foraging, carry a good field guide. I recommend Roger Phillips' *Wild Flowers of Britain* and his *Mushrooms and other Fungi*. I have purposefully chosen only plants which are common, easy to recognise and which cannot be confused with anything poisonous, but it is still important to ensure you pick the right thing.

Gather wild foods on a dry day only where you are allowed, and away from fields sprayed with chemicals. Handle the plants as little as possible, putting them in paper bags or a wicker basket, and eat them as soon as you can. Only pick lightly and where there is a great profusion of the plant, using a pair of secateurs or scissors.

Build up a wild food map of your area, so that the next year you can return to rediscover things you liked. Pick a specimen of each plant and press it between two pieces of clean paper under some heavy books for a few weeks, then mount it in a journal, with its name, a record of the date and where it was found.

3

SPRING PLANTS
spinach greens, shoots, stems and salad plants

Wild greens are at their best in March, April and May, when the young leaves are sweet and tender. These plants have been eaten since the earliest times – it is only in the last hundred years or so so that we have narrowed our tastes solely down to cultivated vegetables. In many other countries, however, people still gather wild greens.

Many of these plants are powerful spring tonics and will give a good boost to the system, especially when eaten in salad. Include a variety of these 'pot-herbs' for a spinach-type mixture, or add them to soups and stews, stir-fries, omelettes, quiches, sauces, sandwiches and spreads.

ALEXANDERS (*Smyrnium olusatrum*). Also known as *Horse Parsley, Black Lovage* or *Wild Celery*. A 3-4 ft high yellow-green plant abundant on the coast. Use the leaves in white sauce, in soups, or battered and deep-fried. The lower pink part of the stems can be steamed and eaten like asparagus. The upper part of the root can be cooked like parsnip and the flower-buds can be used in a salad. [op.]

BISTORT (*Polygonum bistorta*). Also known as *Adderwort, Oderwort, Snakeweed* or *Twice-Writhen*, it grows in moist meadows. Plant in the spring, dividing roots in the Autumn. Enjoys partial shade. Harvest leaves before flowering. A spring tonic herb, traditionally used in the making of herb puddings. Use like spinach and also in soups. [op.]

BORAGE (*Borago officinalis*). Used by the ancient Greeks and Romans. The cucumber-flavoured leaves are cleansing and nutritious, high in potassium and calcium. Add them and the bright blue flowers to salads. Attractive in the garden by a sunny wall. [op.]

Spring Plants

BRACKEN (*Pteris aquilina*). Moor and heathland. Steam or fry the youngest curled-up fronds. Tastes of almonds. [5]

BULLRUSH (*Typha latifolia*). Also known as *Cat-Tail* or *Greater Reedmace*, this common water's edge plant is a treasure. The spring shoots can be added to stir fries. The young flowering shoot is like asparagus. Later, the young flower head can be cooked like corn on the cob. If mature, its pollen can be used as flour. The insides of the cooked roots can be roasted and taste like sweet chestnuts. [op.]

BURDOCK (Lesser) (*Arctium minus*). Eat the youngest leaves as spinach or in salads. Strip the stems and eat in salads or steamed like asparagus. One of the best blood purifiers and tonics. [9]

CHICKWEED (*Stellaria media*). Cook the whole plant as a spinach vegetable, and add to soups. Add the young leaves to salads. Traditionally eaten to build up the blood and strengthen the heart. [op.]

DANDELION (*Taraxacum officinale*). Use as a spinach vegetable, and in salads, and torn into sandwiches with salt and pepper. If you grow dandelions for food, remove the flower heads. To blanch and lessen the bitterness, cover with a plant pot and straw. Perfect for early salads. A powerful blood cleanser and spring tonic. [op.]

EVENING PRIMROSE (*Oenothera biennis*). A large plant found on dunes. Use leaves and flowers in salads, or cook the roots. [15]

FAT HEN & **GOOD KING HENRY** (*Chenopodium album/bonus-henricus*). Delicious spinach-like vegetables, eaten for over 2000 years. Use in soups and stews. Grow in the kitchen garden. [op.]

DANDELION

CHICKWEED

FAT HEN

BULLRUSH

7

Spring Plants

GROUND ELDER (*Aegopodium podagraria*). Also known as *Bishopsweed*, *Gout Weed* and *Herb Gerard*. Cook as spinach. [13]

HAWTHORN (*Crataegus monogyna*). Also *May Tree* or *Bread and Cheese Tree*. Add young shoots to salads for a nice nutty flavour. [29]

HOP (*Humulus lupulus*). Steam the young leaf shoots. [op.]

LADYS MANTLE (*Alchemilla filicaulis*). Found on grassland and open woods. Use the young fresh leaves in salad. [op.]

LADYS SMOCK (*Cardamine pratensis*). Also known as *Cuckoo Flower* or *Bittercress*. Rich in vitamins and minerals. An old cultivated salad herb with a flavour similar to Watercress. Found beside streams, in damp meadows and in woodlands. Pale lilac flowers. An attractive garden plant which will self-seed once established. [op.]

MALLOW (*Malva sylvestris*). Widespread on hedgebanks and waysides. Purple flowers July to September. The leaves are used in making a popular middle eastern soup called *mouloukhia*. [17]

NETTLE (Stinging) (*Urtica dioica*). Use the young spring tops in nettle soup, nettle beer, and nettle pudding. A powerful tonic. [15]

ORACHE (*Atriplex patula*). 'Iron root'. Delicious leaves. [15]

RAMSOMS OR **WILD GARLIC** (*Allium ursinum*). With its white flowers it grows in woods and damp shady places. There is a strong smell of garlic wherever it grows. The long juicy leaves can be used in large quantities raw in salads and sandwiches, or cooked. [59]

ROCK SAMPHIRE (*Crithmum maritimum*). Best from midsummer until September. Common along the coast. Pick the whole plant. Wash in running water before boiling. Serve with butter. [27]

BURDOCK

LADYS MANTLE

HOP

LADYS SMOCK

Spring Plants

RED VALERIAN (*Centranthus ruber*). A common edible wall plant with a pleasant taste. Add the small leaves to salads. The larger ones can be cooked. [op.]

SALAD BURNET (*Sanguisorba minor*). A native meadow salad plant, easily found in the summer by its unusual dark red flowers (a bit like a raspberry). Good in gardens. Eat the young cucumber-flavoured leaves, adding to salads or as a garnish for potatoes. [op.]

SEABEET OR **SEA SPINACH** (*Beta vulgaris*). Common on sea-shores and coastal paths. Strip leaves from the stem. Wash well. [13]

SHEPHERDS PURSE (*Capsella bursa-pastoris*). Also known as *Pepper & Salt* and *Mother's Heart*. A common cress with white flowers and heart-shaped seed cases. The leaves have an aromatic taste. [op.]

SORREL (*Rumex acetosa*). A well-known spinach vegetable, it is always easy to find its small arrowheaded leaves in the spring. Adds a sharp lemony taste to salads, is good in a spinach mix, or made into a traditional French soup. High in oxalic acid – do not overeat. [13]

TANSY (*Tanacetum vulgare*). A vigorous perennial with yellow button flowers, found in hedgerows, meadows and waste ground. Traditionally the young leaves were used at Easter in puddings, cakes and in egg dishes. They are very bitter, use sparingly. [17]

WOOD-SORREL (*Oxalis acetosella*). A salad vegetable in the 14th century, and an attractive plant to grow in shaded areas of the garden. The leaves may be added to salads and soups. A sharp but delicate flavour, not to be over-used (high in oxalic acid). [op.]

WOOD SORREL

SALAD BURNET

RED VALERIAN

SHEPHERDS PURSE

11

SPRING RECIPES

Combining different spring leaves brings a variety of tastes and textures. Like all greens, a huge pile of leaves is reduced to a small heap when cooked, so pick plenty. All recipes serve 4 people.

BASIC COOKED GREENS: Wash 1 lb of leaves, and cook them gently without water in a saucepan with a lid for about five minutes. Drain off the liquid, saving it for soups, by pressing the leaves with the back of a wooden spoon. Season and add a knob of butter. Cover and leave to stand for a few minutes before serving.

SPRING GREENS TORTILLA: In a large frying pan heat olive oil and add 3 chopped onions, sliced garlic and 1 lb diced cooked potatoes. Add cooked chopped greens and pour 4 beaten eggs over the top. Season. Turn the heat right down and put a lid on. Leave for about 5 minutes. Turn upside down onto a plate, re-oil the pan and slide back into the pan to cook the other side. Serve hot or cold.

BASIC PASTRY RECIPE: 6 oz self-raising flour. Rub in 3 oz. margarine until breadcrumbed. Stir in a splash of cold water and work lightly with a fork until it holds together.

BASIC QUICHE RECIPE: Roll pastry onto a floured board to fit a well-oiled pie or flan dish. Into this pastry case add 2 chopped medium fried onions, slices of garlic and 2 oz grated cheese. Add herbs, salt and black pepper. Pour over 4–5 beaten eggs, sprinkle with cheese and bake in the oven for 30 mins, Gas 5, 375°F, 190°C.

SPRING GREENS CHEESE BAKE: Mix 1 lb cooked finely chopped greens, 4 oz cottage cheese, 2 oz grated cheese and three beaten eggs into a pastry lined dish. Bake at medium for half an hour.

SORREL

SPRING RECIPES

GROUND ELDER

SEABEET

Spring Recipes

BASIC SOUP RECIPE: Begin by frying 2-3 chopped onions and sliced garlic. Add a handful of flour and cook for a few minutes. Remove from the heat. In a pan of water add a litre of vegetable stock, seasonings, herbs and vegetables. Bring to the boil. Add the fried onions and flour mixture and cook until the vegetables are soft. The soup may then be liquidized or broken up with a potato masher. For extra flavour add a teaspoon each of curry paste, tahini and soya sauce. Serve with a swirl of cream on the top.

NETTLE SOUP: Use the recipe above, adding sliced potatoes and washed nettle tops. Best liquidized, with nutmeg and cream added.

HERB SOUP: Add a cupful each of chopped wild garlic, wintercress, chickweed and sorrel to the basic recipe.

HERB PUDDING: Traditionally made in the spring. In a muslin bag, lay alternate layers of wild greens (bistort, sorrel and nettle tops are best) and a cereal (medium oatmeal or barley are traditional, but I like rice). Add a little salt and pepper between the layers. Tie the whole thing up and boil for half an hour until the grain has swelled, the leaves have shrunk and the flavours have mingled. Turn out onto a dish of beaten eggs, which instantly cook in the heat, or onto a bed of chopped hard boiled eggs.

SANDWICH SPREAD: Mix chopped leaves with cream cheese or peanut butter. Try borage, ramsoms, sorrel or lady's smock.

WILD GARLIC RELISH: Boil a parsnip, a carrot and an apple. Chop a red onion, a tomato and some wild garlic. Liquidize together in pickling vinegar with seasonings and a little sugar. Preserve in jars.

NETTLE

ORACHE

EVENING PRIMROSE

15

SPRING RECIPES

BASIC BATTER RECIPE: Beat some eggs. Add three tablespoons each of milk, water and plain flour per egg. Add a little salt. Gradually add water until it is smooth and creamy. Leave to stand for at least half an hour. Rebeat just before you use it. For pancakes the batter should be like single pouring cream. For leaf, flower, vegetable and fruit fritters make a slightly thicker mixture.

TANSY PANCAKES: To the basic batter recipe add orange rind, one chopped fresh tansy leaf per egg, and some cream and sherry. In a very hot frying pan add some oil and pour in some of the pancake mixture. As soon as the pancake loosens, turn and cook the other side. Serve with squeezed oranges, sugar, honey, cream or yoghurt.

STEMS AND YOUNG SHOOTS: Tie in bundles with cotton thread, steam quickly and serve with butter and black pepper.

HERB DRESSING: Dice a clove of garlic. Add a teaspoon of chopped mixed herbs, 3 tablespoons of olive oil, lemon juice and a half a teaspoon of Dijon mustard.

HONEY DRESSING: Two tablespoons of olive oil, one each of lemon juice and wine vinegar, half a tablespoon of clear runny honey.

GARLIC DRESSING: With a pestle and mortar crush 4–5 cloves of garlic to a creamy consistency. Add a spoonful of Dijon mustard, olive oil, salt and pepper. Perfect with spring green salad.

YOGHURT DRESSING: Chop a mixture of savoury herbs with some yoghurt and a squeeze of lemon juice.

TAHINI DRESSING: Mix tahini and water to make a paste. Add a squeeze of lemon and a crushed garlic clove.

TANSY

PRIMROSE

VIOLET

COMMON MALLOW

SUMMER
wild flowers and herbs

The summer months are the traditional time to gather wild herbs. They are useful additions to salads and summer pies and are also worth gathering, hanging up to dry and storing for the winter months, when they can be lavishly added to soups and stews. Wild herbs have less flavour than cultivated herbs so you need more of them. They are very hardy and can easily be grown in your garden for a wealth of different flavours to add to your cooking.

Flowers are also a source of food at this time of year. They can be added to salads and fruit salads, and make stunning garnishes. Use them for a spark of unusual colour or flavour. Try nibbling flowers on a walk, but never overpick them from the wild. Growing them yourself is best, as they need to be used fresh and you are then not robbing from the wild.

Many of the mushrooms, nuts and fruits discussed in the Autumn section of this book also begin to appear in the late summer.

BROOM (*Cytisus scoparius*). Flowers March to June. Add the buds to salads, or toss into stir-fry vegetables at the last minute. [27]

BORAGE (*Borago officinalis*). Flowers midsummer. Add the bright blue flowers to salads, fruits salads or fruit cups. Good candied. [5]

CRAB APPLE (*Malus sylvestris*). Flowers mid to late spring. Add to salads. They can also be candied. [op.]

CHAMOMILE (*Chamaemelum nobile*). Flowers midsummer to autumn. A refreshing, calming and soothing tea. [op.]

CRAB APPLE

HAIRY BITTER CRESS

SUMMER

LEMON BALM

CHAMOMILE

SUMMER FLOWERS

ELDER   (*Sambucus nigra*).   A lovely native tree with white sweet–smelling clusters of flowers which appear in the late spring.   Use for herbal tea, cordial, champagne and wine.   Batter and deep fry the whole flower head!   Sprinkle flowers into salads and fruit salads. [op.]

HAWTHORN   (*Crataegus monogyna*).   A common native tree, flowering May to June.   Sprinkle into salads, fruit salads and fruit cups. Use for making wine, liqueur, and a refreshing herbal tea. [29]

LIME   (*Tilia vulgaris*).   Flowers midsummer.   For herbal tea. [op.]

MARIGOLD   (*Calendula officinalis*).   Flowers in August.   Add petals to salads and soups (keep too for the winter).   A good herbal tea. [25]

NASTURTIUM   (*Tropaeolum majus*).   Also known as *Indian Cress*, it flowers from midsummer to autumn.   Add the nutritious leaves, flowers and buds to salads, stirfries and sandwiches.   Batter the flower and deep fry.   A spicy, cress–like flavour and a stunning garnish. [25]

PANSY   (*Viola tricolor*)   **& PRIMROSE**   (*Primula vulgaris*).   Use in salads and as a garnish.   Both can be candied or frittered. [29, 17]

RED CLOVER   (*Trifolium pratense*).   Found growing in the grass, flowering May to September.   Use in salads and battered. [op.]

VIOLET (sweet) (*Violata ordorata*).   Flowers in the spring.   Good in salads, fruits salads, and for flavouring rice dishes and puddings. [17]

WILD ROSE   (*Rosa canina*).   Also known as *Dog Rose*.   For salads, rose petal jam, and wine.   They can also be candied. [op.]

WILD STRAWBERRY   (*Fragaria vesca*).   Found on dry grassland and in woods.   Delicious small fruits appear from June onwards. [31]

ELDER

WILD ROSE

LIME

RED CLOVER

Summer Herbs

HAIRY BITTERCRESS (*Cardamine hirsuta*). Use the leaves and flowers from the middle of the plant. Good spicy cress flavour for salads and sandwich spreads. Found on scrub and walls. [19]

JACK BY THE HEDGE (*Alliaria petiolata*). Also known as *Hedge Garlic*, or *Garlic Mustard*. For a mild garlic flavour add to almost anything. Found in hedgerows and woodland edges. [op.]

LEMON BALM (*Melissa officinalis*). Lemon taste. A long naturalised garden escape. Use in salads, puddings and summer drinks. [19]

MARJORAM (*Origanum vulgare*). A native perennial, common on pasture, hedgebanks and scrub. Use with tomato and pasta. [op.]

MARSH SAMPHIRE (*Salicornia europaea*). Also known as *Glasswort*, it looks likes a miniature cactus. Excellent flavour. Common in salt marshes and tidal mudflats all around the coast. [29]

MINT (APPLE-SCENTED) (*Mentha rotundifolia*), found in hedgerows. Also **WATERMINT** (*Mentha aquatica*), found in streams and ditches. Use in drinks, fruit salads and salads. [25, 31]

ROCK SAMPHIRE (*Crithmum maritimum*). See page 8. [27]

SEA PURSLANE (*Halimone portulacoides*). A native shrub of marshes, estuaries and estuarine rivers. Steam the fleshy leaves. [27]

THYME (wild) (*Thymus vulgaris*). Native on sandy heaths and grassland. Add to soups, stews, salads, egg and tomato dishes. [op.]

WILD FENNEL (*Foeniculum vulgare*). Found on dry soil near the sea. Add leaves to salads, egg and fish dishes. Use the leaves fresh in sandwiches. Add the seeds to bread. Avoid the bulb. [op.]

THYME

JACK BY THE HEDGE

WILD FENNEL

MARJORAM

Summer Recipes

Herbs and flowers can be added to salads, fruit salads, sauces, cakes, bread, nut roasts, quiches, stir-fries, vegetable and fruit flans, omelettes, salad dressings, oils and vinegars, soups and casseroles. As a general rule add herbs at the beginning for soups and casseroles, and near the end for sauces and stir fries. Edible flowers make a wonderful splash of colour and lend an interesting taste. Use them for garnishes and float them in summer drinks.

HERB AND FLOWER BUTTERS: Chop some herbs. Add lemon juice, salt and pepper. Beat into the butter until it is a smooth paste.

RISOTTO OF HERBS AND FLOWERS: In a frying pan gently fry a medium onion and slices of garlic in olive oil. Add a cup of rice and cook briefly. Remove from the heat and add two cups of vegetable stock and half a glass of wine. Simmer until most of the liquid is absorbed and the rice is tender. Stir in a cup of finely chopped herbs and flowers, and add black pepper. Cover and let the pan stand for 2-3 minutes without further heat. Serve with a drizzle of olive oil and a garnish of freshly picked flowers.

BASIC WHITE SAUCE RECIPE: Heat 4 tablespoons of olive oil in a pan and add 3 tablespoons of plain flour. Roast on medium heat, turning constantly until golden. Remove from heat and very gradually add a pint of milk, and some water mixed with half a stock cube. Occasionally return to the heat, and keep stirring constantly as you add the milk, until smooth and creamy. Season to taste.

HERB SAUCE: To the basic white sauce add half a cup of chopped herbs and a tablespoon of soya sauce just before serving.

SUMMER
RECIPES

NASTURTIUM

MARIGOLD

APPLEMINT

SUMMER RECIPES

HERB FLAN/QUICHE: Line a flan dish with pastry (*see page 12*). Into this sprinkle a cup of chopped herbs and flowers, 4 oz of grated cheese, two chopped fried onions and some garlic. Pour in 3-4 eggs mixed with a little milk. Sprinkle with black pepper and cheese and bake in a medium oven for 30 minutes. Serve with salad.

HERBAL VINEGARS AND OILS: Use aromatic herbs or edible flowers. Remove stalks and bases from flowers. Loosely fill a wide-necked jar with fresh herbs/flowers and pour in warmed wine vinegar or olive oil until full. Place in a sunny window and shake daily for two weeks. Strain off the herbs/flowers and rebottle. For salad dressings and marinades. Use flower vinegars on fruit salad.

ROSE PETAL JELLY: Dissolve 2 cups of sugar in half a cup of water. Add a tablespoon each of orange juice and lemon juice, and 2 cups of packed wild rose petals. Cook gently, stirring continuously for half an hour until the petals have melted. Cool, then pour into a jam jar and keep cold. For yoghurt, ice cream, pancakes and waffles.

CANDIED FLOWERS: Remove stalks and bases. Beat an egg-white until foamy. Dip each flower or petal in egg-white, then in sugar. Place on greaseproof paper on a cooling rack. When full, cover with a new sheet and leave in a very low oven with open door until dry. Store in an airtight container. For dessert decorations.

BASIC FLOWER LIQUEUR RECIPE: Pack the petals into a wide-necked bottle. Sprinkle in 2-3 tablespoons of sugar and fill with brandy, vodka or gin. Cork. Shake daily for 3 weeks. Strain off the flowers and rebottle. Try May blossom, rosepetals or elderflowers.

ROCK SAMPHIRE

BROOM

SEA PURSLANE

SUMMER RECIPES

SUMMER FLOWER AND HERB TEAS: Pour a pint of boiling water onto at least 6 or 7 sprigs of herbs or flowers (tie them in a bunch for easy removal). Cover and leave for 5 minutes. Remove leaves and flowers. Add honey, sugar or lemon juice. Can be served chilled with ice and slices of lemon. Experiment!

MOROCCAN MINT TEA: Bring a pint of water to the boil in a pan. Add 7 sprigs of mint, cover and simmer for 5 minutes. Strain into a jug. Stir in 5 teaspoons of sugar. Sweet and delicious.

ELDERFLOWER CORDIAL: In a large bowl put ten elderflower heads, $1\frac{1}{2}$lbs of sugar, 2 chopped lemons and 1 oz of tartaric acid. Pour on 4 pints of boiling water. Stir well. Cover with a tea towel and leave for 24 hours, stirring occasionally. Strain through muslin and then bottle. Can be used straight away or kept for a few weeks (or longer if the bottles are sterilised and corked). Dilute with water.

FLOWER FRITTERS: Using the basic batter recipe (*on page 16*) dip summer flowers into the batter and then drop into hot oil. Deep fry until golden – just a couple of minutes. Drain onto kitchen towel and serve with sugar and cream. Try elderflower heads, nasturtium, wild rose petals, pansies and red clover heads.

CREAMY TOMATO HERB SAUCE: Fry 2 chopped onions and some sliced garlic in olive oil. Remove from heat and add a tin of chopped tomatoes, 2 tablespoons or more of chopped herbs, 2 tablespoons of soya sauce, a small tub or packet of cream (or soya cream) and some black pepper. Cook for 5 minutes. Good with fish and pasta dishes.

PANSY

HAWTHORN

MARSH
SAMPHIRE

29

SUMMER RECIPES

Many fruits, nuts and mushrooms (*see the Autumn section of this book*) can first be found during August. The first pickings of wild fruit can be made into that classic old favourite:

SUMMER PUDDING: Rinse a pudding basin with cold water and line it with bread, leaving no gaps. Cook 2 lbs of mixed wild fruit for a few minutes in 2-3 tablespoons of water and 3 tablespoons of sugar. Strain off a cupful of the juice, pour the rest into the lined basin. Cover with bread. Put a plate and a weight on the top and leave over-night. In the morning invert the pudding over a plate and pour over the remaining fruit juice. Serve with cream.

FRUIT JELLY: Bring 1 pint of apple juice to the boil and add a pint of raspberries or any wild fruit. Add 2 tablespoons of agar agar. Simmer for 5 mins. Pour into a dish. Add more fruit when cool.

FRUIT SAUCE: Cook any chopped seasonal fruit in a little water. Simmer for 5 minutes with the lid on. Thicken with a little diluted arrowroot and add sugar or honey. Pour over yogurt or ice-cream.

FLOWER SUGARS: Alternately place castor sugar and fresh flowers or herbs in a dry lidded jar. Do not fill. Shake daily for 2 weeks, then sieve out the flowers and dry the sugar in the oven set at a low temperature. store in a dark airtight container. Use to flavour cakes, biscuits, desserts, etc. Try roses, violets, lavender or thyme.

PICKLED WALNUTS: Pick the young green nuts in July. Prick with a fork and leave them covered in strong brine for a week, until they are black. Drain, wash and dry them for two days. Pack into jars, covering with hot pickling vinegar. Seal and eat after a month.

WATER MINT

WALNUT

WILD STRAWBERRY

AUTUMN
edible hedgerow fruit

As we pass from high summer into autumn, the hedgerows are rich with fruits. These make tasty wayside snacks, or can be stewed in a pan on the camp fire. Fruits can be brought home for pies, crumbles, sauces and purées. They can also be preserved for the months ahead in jams, jellies, fruit cheeses, chutneys, cordials, wines and liqueurs.

BILBERRY (*Vaccinium myrtilis*). Also known as *Whortleberry*, *Huckleberry* and *Blueberry*. A low shrub, found on heaths and moors. Good for jam using $\frac{1}{2}$ lb of sugar to 1 lb berries. Eat raw or cook with sugar, lemon juice and peel. Use in pies, open tarts, and on pancakes. Native Americans dried them for winter soups and stews. [op.]

BLACKBERRY (*Rubus fruticosus*). Everyone's favourite. Eat them raw with sugar and cream, or bake them into pies and crumbles. Mix them with stewed apple. Make jam, jelly, wine and vinegar. [op.]

BULLACE (*Prunus insititia*). *Wild damson*. Leave on the tree until the first frosts have reduced their acidity. Pies, jams and wines. [39]

CHERRY PLUM (*Prunus cerasifera*). A small tree, found in hedgerows or woods. Use the yellow fruit in pies, jams & liqueurs. [op.]

CRAB APPLE (*Malus sylvestris*). Common in hedgerows. Small golden apples from Sept. Jelly, wine, cider, verjuice & cheese. [35]

DAMSON (*Prunus domesticus*). Found in autumn and early winter hedgerows. Wonderful for pies, jams, pickles, wine and cheese. [op.]

ELDERBERRY (*Sambucus nigra*). A small hedgerow tree with drooping clusters of black berries. Makes jam, jelly, cordial, wine, vinegar and chutney. Mixed with stewed apples and other fruit. [41]

CHERRY PLUM

BILBERRY

AUTUMN

BLACKBERRY

DAMSON

Autumn Fruits

GEULDER ROSE (*Viburnum opulus*). Also known as *Snowball tree, Red elder, Rose elder, High cranberry, Whitsun rose* and *Cramp bark*. A native shrub found in damp hedgerows, woods and copses. Fruits in August and September. Too bitter to eat raw but may be cooked as a substitute for cranberries, and made into a sharp jelly. [op.]

HAWTHORN (*Crateagus monogyna*). The haws can be made into wine, conserve, haw brandy, and dried for fruit tea. [39]

JUNIPER (*Juniperus communis*). A native evergreen shrub of chalk downs, limestone hills, heath and moorland. The fruit ripens in its second or third year so only pick the soft black ones. Add to other fruit for pies and jam. Can be dried and added to soup and stew in the winter. Can be made into juniper gin. [37]

MEDLAR (*Mespilus germanica*). Once a popular fruit. Pick in early November after the first frosts have turned the fruit from yellow to brown and they have become soft ('blet'). Bake quickly in the oven and eat the soft fruit with cream. Makes a good jelly and cheese. [41]

ROSEHIP (*Rosa canina*). Use the bright red berries of the common wild rose to make rosehip syrup, soup, purée and wine. [41]

ROWAN (*Sorbus aucuparia*). *Mountain ash.* A small attractive tree with clusters of orange-red berries. Good for wine. It also makes an excellent jelly – add some chopped crab apples to ensure it sets. [37]

SLOE (*Prunus spinosa*). *Blackthorn.* Oct. to Nov. Pick after the first frost. Beware the thorns! For jelly, wine and sloe gin. [39]

WILD GOOSEBERRY and **RASPBERRY** (*Ribes uva-crispa & Rubus ideaus*). Woods and hedgerows. July to September. [op., 37]

GUELDER ROSE

CRAB APPLE

AUTUMN

WILD GOOSEBERRY

Autumn Fruit Recipes

BASIC STEWED FRUIT OR FRUIT PUREE RECIPE: Wash the fruit and simmer gently in a little water, sugar or honey to taste. Keep the lid on the pan to keep the flavours in. A bunch of sweet cicely will reduce the amount of sugar needed. To make a fruit purée, sieve to remove seeds and skins. Beat to a smooth paste. Alternatively, fruit can be stewed in a covered pan with a little butter.

FRUIT FOOL: Mix cold sweet purée and whipped double cream (or cream and yoghurt). Serve chilled with a flower or fruit garnish.

FRUIT FLAN: Line a pie dish with sweet pastry (add 2 oz sugar to basic recipe on page 12). Bake for 15 mins in a medium oven. Chop fruit into thin slices and lay in the crust. Make a honey and water syrup, thickened with arrowroot, agar agar or fruit purée. Bring to the boil and pour over the fruit. Serve with cream.

CRAB APPLE JELLY: Chop 2 lbs of crab apples. Just cover with cold water, adding ginger slices and half a lemon to taste. Simmer until the fruit is pulped. Pour the pulp into a jelly bag or sieve lined with muslin to drip overnight (do not squeeze or your jelly will be cloudy). Measure and add 1 lb of sugar for each pint of juice. Stir over a low heat and then rapid boil until the mixture shows signs of setting when dribbled onto a cold plate. Pour into sterilised jam jars. Leave to set. Cover with greaseproof paper rounds and seal.

BLACKBERRY AND APPLE JELLY: Made by the same method, using equal amounts of cooking apples and blackberries.

HEDGEROW JELLY: Combine an assortment of hedgerow fruits with half the amount of crab or cooking apples to help it set.

RASPBERRY

ROWAN

JUNIPER

Autumn Fruit Recipes

ROWANBERRY JELLY: Use a mixture of 2 parts rowan berries to 1 part crab or cooking apples. Make in the usual way (*see page 36*).

FRUIT CHEESE: Wash and rough cut crab apples and other fruit (medlars, quinces, elderberries or damsons). Add water to a third of the way up the fruit. Boil until soft. Rub through a sieve and weigh the pulp. Return to a clean pan with an equal weight of sugar. Bring slowly to the boil, stirring in the sugar, then hard boil for at least an hour. Setting point is reached when the mixture forms soft balls when dropped into cold water. Spread into an oiled baking tin and leave to set. Cut into chunks and wrap in waxed paper. Store in a cool place. Serve with cheese or diced and dusted with icing sugar.

ELDERBERRY AND APPLE JAM: Quick and easy and a firm favourite. Make a pulp by boiling 2 lbs of rough chopped apples in some water, and pass through a sieve to remove seeds, core and skin. Do the same with 2 lbs of elderberries (just a little water needed). Combine the two pulps, adding 4 lbs of sugar, and boil for about ten minutes until it thickens. Makes seven jars of jam.

SLOE GIN: Prick one pint of sloes and put them into a wide-necked jar. Sprinkle in 2 oz of sugar and top up with gin or vodka. Cork and shake daily for three months. Strain off the fruit and rebottle. Leave for a year if you can resist the temptation! Trim the gin-soaked sloes from the stones and add to melted chocolate or fruit cake. Make other fruit liqueurs in the same way with damsons, bullace, crab apples or juniper berries.

HAW BRANDY: A traditional liqueur made by the same method as sloe gin with hawthorn berries and brandy.

HAWTHORN

SLOES

BULLACE

39

Autumn Fruit Recipes

BLACKBERRY CORDIAL: Pour one pint of wine vinegar over 2 lbs blackberries. Cover with a tea towel and let it stand for a week, stirring often. Strain and bring to a strong boil, adding 1 lb of sugar and $\frac{1}{2}$ lb of honey. When cool bottle and keep in the dark.

ROSEHIP SYRUP: Add 2 lbs of rough chopped rosehips to 4 pints of boiling water. Bring to the boil and remove from the heat. Cover and let stand for 30 minutes. Strain through muslin. Keep the liquid and return the pulp to the pan with another 4 pints of boiling water. Repeat. Combine the liquids in a clean pan and boil, reducing by half. Remove from heat and dissolve 2 lb sugar. Return to heat and hard boil for 5 mins. Pour into warmed sterilised bottles.

BLACKBERRY SYRUP: Stew 3 lbs with a quarter pint of water. Strain. For every pint of juice add 6 oz of sugar. Boil for 15 minutes and bottle. You can also combine blackberries and elderberries.

ELDERBERRY CHUTNEY: Stalk and wash 2 lbs of elderberries. Put them in a pan and bruise them with a wooden spoon. Add a large chopped onion, 1 pint of vinegar and 2 tablespoon of sugar. Add 1 teaspoon each of salt, ground ginger and mustard seeds, and half a teaspoon each of cayenne pepper and mixed spice. Bring to the boil and simmer until it becomes thick. Put into warmed jars when cool.

PICKLED DAMSONS: Tie in a muslin bag: 1 small cinnamon stick, 1 blade of mace, $\frac{1}{2}$ oz allspice, a small ginger root, chopped rind of half a lemon. Gently boil with half a pint of white vinegar, 1 lb demerara sugar, and 2 lbs firm slightly underripe damsons. When the fruit is just tender carefully pile into jars. Fierce boil the liquid until it thickens and pour over the fruit. Close tightly.

MEDLAR

ROSE HIPS

ELDER

ALMOND

41

Nuts and Seeds

Nuts and seeds can be dried and stored for winter use. Nuts are best stored in their shells. Check for any insect holes! Dried seeds are bruised with a pestle and mortar before use.

Acorns (*Quercus robur*). Excellent oak 'coffee'. Roast the peeled kernels in a heavy frying pan until golden. Grind and roast again. [45]

Almond (*Prunus dulcis*). Nuts can be found in the South. Use in cakes and biscuits. Grind them to make a flour. [41]

Cleavers (*Galium aparine*). The seeds may be roasted in a pan for an excellent coffee substitute. [op.]

Common Red Poppy (*Papaver rhoeas*). Shake dry seed heads into paper bags. Sprinkle on bread, cakes and cream cheese. [op.]

Fennel (*Foeniculum vulgare*). Add the seeds to bread sauces, stir fries and stews. Also use to make a wonderful tea to aid digestion. [45]

Hazel (*Corylus avellana*). Eat the green nuts raw. Use them dried in cakes, biscuits, nut butters, spreads, nut roasts and nut burgers. [op.]

Mallow (*Malva sylvestris*). Seeds known as 'cheeses'. [17]

Nasturtium (*Tropaeolum majus*). Harvest in September. Add the seeds to salads or pickle them in vinegar to resemble capers. [45]

Sweet Chestnut (*Castanea sativa*). Slit the inner shell and roast by a fire or on a shovel nearby. They may be boiled, skinned and made into purée, chestnut stuffing, burgers and soup. [op.]

Walnut (*Juglans regia*). October to November. Use in savoury recipes like stir-fry vegetables, tomato pasta dishes, or in salad dishes with rice. Bake in cakes. Pickle them when green (*page 30*). [41]

COMMON RED POPPY

HAZEL

SWEET CHESTNUT

CLEAVERS

Nut Recipes

Roasted Nuts: Spread on an oiled tray and bake for 10 mins at 190°C, or gently fry in a little oil, adding soya sauce when golden.

Hazelnut Butter: Grind 8 oz (225g) of salted roasted hazelnuts and mix to a paste with 3 oz (75g) of butter.

Chocolate Hazelnut Spread: To the above recipe add 4 oz (110g) of melted dark chocolate or smooth paste of dark cocoa!

Nut Roast: Combine 2 or 3 chopped fried onions with 4 oz rough chopped nuts. Add 4 oz of rice, breadcrumbs or oats. Bind together with 1 lb of puréed or diced vegetables, tomato pureé and a vegetable stock cube mixed into half a pint of water to make a soft mixture. Add seeds, spices, herbs and soya sauce to taste and pile it into an oiled pie dish. Press firmly down and bake at 180°C for 45 minutes. Diced cheese and beaten eggs can also be added to bind it.

Nut Burgers: Use the same type of mixture. Shape on a floured board. Fry for 5 minutes each side on a low to medium heat.

Walnut Balls: Combine ground walnuts, breadcrumbs, grated cheese, grated onion, a diced red pepper, chopped parsley, seasoning, and a beaten egg. Form into balls, then bake or fry.

Chestnut Jam: Boil 2 lb chestnuts for 30 minutes after slitting both sides. Peel, skin and sieve them to make a syrup with half a pint of water, $1\frac{1}{2}$ lbs of sugar and 3 teaspoons of vanilla. Add the sieved chestnuts and cook until it thickens. Pour into jars.

Chestnut Soup: Sweat an onion, a carrot and diced celery in butter. Add 1 lb peeled cooked chestnuts and a pint of stock. Simmer for 10 mins. Season, liquidise and serve with cream and nutmeg.

FENNEL

OAK

CHESTNUT

AUTUMN
RECIPES

NASTURTIUM

MUSHROOMS & FUNGI

This is an extensive aspect of wild food cookery, and a few common varieties are included here. Please use a good field guide and gather only what you are sure of. My favourite guide is Roger Phillips' *Mushrooms and other Fungi*. Pick mushrooms on a dry day, preferably early in the morning, twisting them off at the base. Bracket fungi need to be cut from the tree with a knife. Check each one for grub infestation by slicing through the stem with a knife, then lay them carefully in a basket. If you wish to gather specimens for identification at home, take a separate basket – never mix these with your edibles.

When you get home check each one carefully and select the best to eat immediately, putting aside the poorer ones for soups or sauces. Eat mushrooms fresh or dry them for winter soups and stews.

BEEFSTEAK FUNGUS (*Fistulina hepatica*). A bracket fungus resembling a slab of meat, found on the sides of old oaks and chestnut trees. Pick the fresh ones from late summer to the first frosts. Slice into 1cm strips which can be fried in butter, covered with stock or wine and simmered for ten minutes. Alternatively, dry the strips. [51]

CEP (*Boletus edulis*). The *Penny Bun*. Common in mixed woodland from late July, especially under conifers. This brown bun-shaped mushroom has a creamy white spongy underside (instead of gills) which turns yellow and no stem ring. A pleasant smell and a mild nutty taste. Only pick the youngest. [op.]

CHANTERELLE (*Cantharellus cibarius*). Found mainly in pine, beech and birch woods from July to December. Yellowy orange, funnel-shaped with no ring, it has a pleasant apricoty smell. Wonderful stewed and added to egg dishes. [op.]

CHANTARELLE

CEP

PUFFBALL

SHAGGY
INK CAP

MUSHROOMS & FUNGI

FIELD & HORSE MUSHROOMS (*Agaricus campester & arvensis*).
Found near woods, fields and pasture. Familiar white mushrooms,
pink gills which darken to brown as they mature. Avoid if they turn
bright yellow or pink when sliced, or if they have white gills. Fry in
butter, or use in pies, soup, sauces, with eggs and with cream. [49]

GIANT PUFFBALL (*Langermannia gigantea*). Woods, fields and
hedges. May be anything from the size of a grapefruit to a football.
Check the flesh is white and fresh. Cut into half inch slices and fry.
Great between slices of bread and in other mushroom dishes. [47]

HORN OF PLENTY (*Craterellus cornucopoides*). Found in leaf litter
in deciduous woods. Light to dark brown. Delicious dried. [51]

JEW'S EAR (*Auricularia auricula*). Common on elder trees in late
autumn. A reddy-brown ear-shaped bracket fungus which grows in
clusters. Cut from the tree with a knife. Slice finely and stew. [51]

OYSTER MUSHROOM (*Pleurotus ostreatus*). Common on dead
ash and beech branches. Slatey silver-grey bracket fungus, the gills are
white and deep, the flesh soft but rubbery. Excellent stewed. [op.]

PARASOL (*Macrolepiota procera/rhacodes*). Found in clearings, beside
woods, meadows and waysides. It has a distinctive ring, a pleasant
smell and nutty flavour. Pick just as the cap begins to open. Good
dipped in batter and deep fried. The stem is too woody to eat. [op.]

SHAGGY INKCAP (*Coprinus comatus*). *Lawyer's Wig.* Common in
fields and waysides. White, covered with shaggy brown scales. Only
pick them young and tightly closed as they quickly go black and
slimey. Cook as soon as possible. Good battered whole. [47]

OYSTER

FIELD MUSHROOM

PARASOL

HORSE MUSHROOM

49

MUSHROOM RECIPES

DRIED MUSHROOMS: Choose only the best quality. Thread and hang them in a warm place (over an Aga or in an airing cupboard) or lay them in baking trays in a very low oven, until they are brittle and snap. Slice larger mushrooms. Store in airtight containers.

FRIED MUSHROOMS: Fry in a mixture of olive oil and butter. Sprinkle with salt to help them sweat. Add garlic and herbs, boiling off any excess liquid. Serve on toast or with eggs with black pepper.

MUSHROOMS IN MILK: Fry 1lb mushrooms in butter, with chopped onions. Add three quarters of a pint of milk and stir while bringing slowly to the boil. Add thyme, salt and pepper, and simmer for 45 minutes. Thicken with some cornflour mixed in water. Pour over toast, potatoes, pasta or root vegetables.

MUSHROOM SAUCE: Liquidize the above recipe.

MUSHROOM SOUP: Fry $\frac{1}{2}$lb mushrooms and 2 onions. Add 1 pint vegetable stock and a little wine. Simmer for 15 mins. Liquidize.

MUSHROOM FRITTERS: Use the basic batter recipe (*page 16*). Wash the mushrooms, and slice or leave whole if unopened. Coat lightly in flour, dip in the batter and deep fry until golden brown.

MUSHROOM POTATO CAKES: Mix cooked mashed potatoes, some milk, butter, grated cheese and diced fresh mushrooms. Knead in enough flour to bind the mixture together. Form into cakes on a floured board and fry until golden brown. Serve with salad.

GREEK MUSHROOMS: Fry onions, mushrooms and plenty of sliced garlic. When soft add chopped tomatoes, thyme, a diced green pepper and half a glass of wine. Cook for 1 minute. Serve cold.

BEEFSTEAK

JEWS EAR

AUTUMN RECIPES

HORN OF PLENTY

ROOTS

It is advisable not to dig too many roots from the wild, as we now try to protect our wild plants. Collect the seeds in Autumn and grow them in your garden. Perhaps in time seeds from your garden will help recolonize the wild. Roots are dug from August onwards and are good until the hard frosts. Some will overwinter.

ALEXANDERS (*Smyrnium olusatrum*). Eat the upper root. [5]

BURDOCK (*Arctium minus*). May be roasted whole, or sliced thinly in stir fries. Used to make dandelion and burdock beer. [op.]

CHICORY (*Cichorium intybus*). *Wild succory*. Common in the south with blue flowers. Boil the roots as a vegetable. Coffee substitute. [op.]

DANDELION (*taraxacum officinale*). Thinly slice the roots for stir fries, soups or stews, make into a coffee substitute. [op.]

EVENING PRIMOSE (*Oenothera biennis*). Grow at the back of a sunny border. Boil the fleshy first year roots. A mild nutty taste. [15]

HORSERADISH (*Armoracia rusticana*). A 3ft plant, common on wasteground and roadsides with a large dock–type leaf. [55]

LOVAGE (*Levisticum officinale*). Aromatic flavoured root vegetable, formerly eaten in the Scottish Highlands. [55]

SALSIFY (*Tragopogon porrifolius*). An old kitchen garden favourite, tasting a bit like salt fish. Steam with butter and lemon juice. [55]

SILVERWEED (*Potentilla anserina*). Abundant in damp grassy places. Good garden ground cover with attractive yellow flowers and silver undersides to the leaf. Boil, slice or bake the roots. [op.]

RED VALERIAN (*Centranthus ruber*). Use the roots for soups. [11]

CHICORY

DANDELION

BURDOCK
ROOT

SILVERWEED

53

ROOT RECIPES

DANDELION & BURDOCK BEER: Scrub large burdock and dandelion roots (2 each). Chop into a pan with 4 pints of water. Boil for 30 minutes. In another pan, gently dissolve 1lb of sugar in 4 pints of water with 2 tablespoons of black treacle and the juice of a lemon. Strain the roots, combine the two liquids and leave to go tepid. Add 1 oz yeast mixed to a paste in warm water. Leave to ferment in a covered bucket for 3-4 days, then bottle. Drink after one week.

HORSERADISH SAUCE: Cut off the skin and grate the white root (outside if possible!). Combine the grated horseradish with yoghurt or double cream, adding some seasoning and sugar, mustard powder and wine vinegar to taste. Great with cheese on toast!

ROOT SALAD: Slice roots to matchstick size. Steam or boil in water. Drain, cool and combine with mayonnaise or vinegar.

ROOT COFFEE: Wash dandelion and/or chicory roots quickly (do not soak). Dry and chop them and spread onto a baking tray. Bake at Gas 2/150°C/300°F until they are brown and brittle, then grind them and keep in a jar. Use in the usual way to make coffee.

ROOT SOUP: Follow the basic soup recipe (*page 14*) adding any available roots, washed and sliced. When the roots are soft liquidize to a creamy consistency and add seasoning.

BAKED SALSIFY: Scrape 1lb salsify roots. Cut up and leave for a few minutes in water with a drop of vinegar. Drain and boil in stock or water until tender. Drain again, keeping the water for the sauce. Make a basic white sauce, adding cheese or herbs and pour over the diced root in an oven dish. Bake in a hot oven for 10 minutes.

LOVAGE

HORSERADISH

AUTUMN
RECIPES

SALSIFY

WINTER

Winter is the time to use all the things you have saved from the year's foraging, adding dried herbs and flowers, mushrooms, nuts and berries to soups and stews, and preserved fruits to puddings.

A few plants can be found in the winter, all of which have been used since ancient times, and are worth encouraging into your garden: **CHICKWEED** (*Stellaria media*), **HAIRY BITTERCRESS** (*Cardamine hirsuta*), **YARROW** (*Achillea millefolium*), **SHEPHERDS PURSE** (*Capsella bursa-pastoris*) and **COMMON WINTERCRESS** (*Yellow rocket*) (*Barbarea vulgaris*). Trim the leaves from the stems.

Some plants can be sown in the Autumn and, protected by cloches and straw, will provide you with fresh leaves throughout the winter: Try **CORN SALAD** (*Valerianella locusta*), **SALAD BURNETT** (*Sanguisorba minor*) and **SORRELL** (*Rumex acestosa*). Treat these as cut-and-come-agains, letting them go to seed in the Spring. **DANDELION** (*Taraxacum officinale*) and **CHICORY** (*Cichorium intybus*) leaves may be forced under plant pots covered with straw.

The roots of **SALSIFY** (*Tragopogon porrifolius*), **JERUSALEM ARTICHOKE** (*Helianthus tuberosus*), **MARSHMALLOW** (*Althaea officinalis*) and **WOOD AVENS** (*Herb bennet*) (*Geum urbanum*) can be left in the ground and dug when needed.

WINTER HOT POT: Soak dried mushrooms in boiling water for half an hour. Fry onions, slices of ginger, bruised cumin and coriander seeds, diced root vegetables and chopped leaves or herbs. Add a little flour. Add a pint of vegetable stock, the mushrooms and nuts and dried berries. Cook gently for an hour, adding seasoning.

WOOD AVENS

WINTER CRESS

WINTER

MARSH MALLOW

CORN SALAD

YARROW

INDEX OF PLANTS

58

INDEX OF RECIPES

ROUGH CONVERSIONS

1lb is half a kilo (450g)
1oz is 28 grams
2oz is 57 grams
4oz is 113 grams
1 pint is 570 millilitres
½ a pint is 285 ml
¼ pint is 140 ml
1 litre is 1¾ pints
1 gallon is 4½ litres
10 fluid oz = 300 ml
18 fluid oz = 500 ml

Oven Temperatures:

Gas 1 = 140°C = 275°F
Gas 2 = 150°C = 300°F
Gas 3 = 170°C = 325°F
Gas 4 = 180°C = 350°F
Gas 5 = 190°C = 375°F
Gas 6 = 200°C = 400°F
Gas 7 = 220°C = 425°F
Gas 8 = 230°C = 450°F
Gas 9 = 245°C = 475°F